D1461734

lolly Woe

Anna Perera

Illustrated by Martina Selway

OXFORD
UNIVERSITY PRESS

Contents

CHAPTER 1

Ouch!

'Watch Lucy while I run to the shops,' Mum yelled. 'And for the tenth time, get that bedroom sorted out!'

The front door slammed shut so hard it shook Albie's glasses half off his nose and dislodged a cornflake from a back tooth. Albie pushed his brown hair out of his eyes, twitched his glasses up his nose to the right position, and idly turned the pages of the *Heveling Weekly News* that was spread out on the kitchen table.

Collect 1000 Lolly Sticks

'Why would anyone do a stupid thing like that?' Albie huffed and read on:

The first four children to collect 1000 lolly sticks with jokes on them will each win a colour television set from Hill's Ice-cream.

Albie sat back and stared into space. A vague, wondering look spread across his face. He needed a television set. Mum had got rid of theirs when they left their last house because the rent was 'getting too much', and the evenings had been dead boring ever since.

'Hmmm!' Albie sat up and read the rules.

Entries must arrive at Hill's Ice-cream Unit, Main Road, Heveling Industrial Estate, no later than July 27th.

Entrants must be no older than 13 years.

All 1000 lolly sticks must have jokes on them.

Jokes can be repeated any number of times.

Name, address and age must be clearly printed on a postcard attached to the bag of lolly sticks.

Hill's Ice-cream Unit accepts no liability for loss of entries.

The judges' decision is final.

Albie narrowed his eyes. He wasn't totally convinced this was something he should be interested in, even though he wanted a television. On the other hand, the summer holidays stretched out in front of him without so much as a single event to look forward to. Then he realized he only had three days to collect a thousand sticks and decided on the spot not to bother. There was no chance he'd win.

'Play wiv me?' Lucy, arms full of purple and silver plastic ponies pushed the kitchen door open. 'Go on!'

'You're almost four, I'm eleven. You woke me up twice last night to tell me your pony had a baby. Waffle dog spent all night licking my ears and smothering me with his smelly breath. You've got to play on your own today. I'm not in the mood!'

'I don't want to,' Lucy sniffed, dropping her ponies on the floor. 'Why should I?'

'Because I said so!' Albie tucked the newspaper under his arm, jumped over the ponies and headed for his tiny bedroom. 'I'll play with you later!' Waffle dog followed him up the stairs, bringing his own special smell with him.

'Horrible brother!' he could hear Lucy calling as he kicked a few socks and computer magazines across the floor and cleared a space on the bed.

Waffle dog immediately occupied it, forcing Albie to perch on an awkward space in the corner. He opened the paper and read about the competition again.

It was tempting to try and win a colour telly. If he was on his own and Lucy got on his nerves he could go off and watch television. Or he could play computer games in peace with his friends. But he didn't have any friends round here! He had only been living in Heveling for two weeks. You couldn't count Tash Ferris who had stopped him in the playground on the last day of school and asked, 'How's it going?'

'Yeah, not bad!' Albie had said, wondering why she was asking.

'I only live four doors down from you!' Tash told him. Albie couldn't figure out how she knew. He told his mum about the conversation. She said: 'Kids notice when kids the same age move nearby. It's one of those things.'

All morning Albie had been wondering whether to knock for Tash. But he was oh so tired and he didn't want her to think he wanted her company. She might get the wrong idea and where would that leave him? No, it was better to sit on the corner of his bed imagining a great big colour television in the room, than it was to knock for Tash Ferris, however nice she seemed. Then he got to thinking about her black, tangly hair, the way her eyes darted about like wriggling tadpoles and her amazing laugh that sounded like a chicken having a nightmare. 'Eeeek, eeeek, eeeeeeeek!' Really, she was quite nice, he decided.

Suddenly there was a bang at the door. Albie clambered over Waffle dog to press his nose against the bedroom window and look down. Standing at the front door was the very person he'd been thinking about. Tash Ferris, hands in

her pockets, stood grinning up at him. Waffle dog's stomach rumbled loudly as Albie flung the catch open.

'Hi!' he shouted down, wafting away the air behind with both hands in case it tornadoed out of the window and hit Tash full in the face.

'Hey,' Tash looked up, not noticing it from where she was standing. 'Want to do something?'

'Er,' Albie hesitated, wondering why she'd come. 'What exactly?'

'Anything!' Tash pulled a face. 'I'm so bored sitting around!'

'Okay,' Albie laughed. 'Come up.' He turned to Waffle, 'And don't you dare do that again!'

He raced down the stairs three at a time and nearly fell flat on his face as he skidded to the front door.

'This way,' Albie said, opening the door and pretending he hadn't almost knocked his teeth out getting there. Tash was about to follow him upstairs when a spotted blue pony with a bright pink mane came flying at her from the living room. She ducked before it smacked her in the face. 'What the—?'

'Lucy!' Albie yelled. 'Stop it!'

'No,' Lucy said as they raced upstairs. 'Why should I? Mum said you had to play wiv me.'

Flying ponies came at them faster than missiles as they ran to Albie's messy bedroom. Albie quickly closed the door. Two ponies hit the door. Smack! Thump! Tash laughed, 'Eeek, eeeeek!'

'I haven't sorted everything out yet.' Albie kicked a grubby T-shirt under the bed.

'Right!' Tash shrugged. 'See you've got Total Race!' She pointed to a computer game on the floor. 'I thought it was quite good at first but now I think it's useless.'

'Yeah, I know,' Albie said. 'Rubbish.' He pretended to agree, surprised she knew about the game. Waffle let out a loud snore. Albie

elbowed his soft stomach to remind him he'd been warned.

Waffle burped instead.

'Does your dog usually sleep on your bed?' Tash asked.

'No,' Albie grinned. 'Only on Saturdays between nine and eleven in the morning. Not that he can tell the time. It's funny the way he knows . . .'

Tash gave him a look which said, I wouldn't

let a big smelly thing like that sleep on my bed. Albie sighed, to let her know it wasn't his idea to have him there. There was an embarrassed silence until Tash rescued the newspaper from the floor.

'What's this? "**Collect 1000 Lolly Sticks**. *The first four children to collect 1000 lolly sticks with jokes on them will each win a colour television set . . .*"' She flashed her wriggling tadpole eyes at him. 'Are you going to do it?'

'Dunno,' Albie shuffled from foot to foot. 'There's only three days left.'

'Go on,' Tash grinned. 'What else is there to do round here?'

Albie smiled a fake smile.

'I can't today. I've got to look after Lucy.' He felt oh so tired and he wasn't sure how you shared a colour television set even if you managed to win one. Why did she want to do it with him anyway? Really, he'd prefer to collect the lolly sticks on his own and he didn't want her to know about it.

'I see,' Tash stared him straight in the eye.

'Scared I might win?'

'No way!' Albie threw his head back. 'As if.' So she was going to do it, was she? Great! Tash saw the look on his face and turned and walked out of the door. She was annoyed. 'Maybe I'll see you later then. I can't breathe in this room with that smelly dog.'

'Where do fleas go in winter?' He shouted after her to try and rescue the situation.

'I don't have that problem,' Tash said sniffily from the hall, diving out the front door as a purple pony with an orange mane hit her splat on her bottom. 'Ouch!'

'"Search me" is the answer,' Albie yelled at the closed door.

'GET OFF MY BED, WAFFLE DOG!' A loud snore rang out. 'You've just ruined my chances of finding a girlfriend!'

CHAPTER 2

Call me a worm?

Albie gazed into nothingness as car lights moved around his bedroom walls. The thin blue curtains were wide open and he could see the full moon from his pillow. Waffle snored for England on the floor beside him, breathing out a smell worse than newly-emptied bins. But even that couldn't wipe out the sight of Tash's wriggling tadpole eyes. The sound of two people walking down the street shouting at each other did, however, invade the thought of her tangly, black hair.

'Arsenal! You're daft!'

'Oh yeah, is that right?'

Albie knelt up in bed and looked out of the window at two teenagers arguing in the middle of the road. They were both sucking orange lollies. One boy slid the lolly stick under his curled up tongue like a spike and then tried to speak. 'Arffenal arrr ruvvish!' he said, pulling the stick out and flicking it away.

Albie grabbed his glasses from the bedside table and pushed them on. Screwing up his eyes, he peered out of the window to see if the lolly stick had a joke on it. He couldn't see. Still dressed in his T-shirt and boxer shorts he ran downstairs and out into the road. By the time he got there the teenagers had gone. Quick as a flash he picked up the lolly stick and ran back inside. Thankful no one had seen him, Albie switched on the hall light.

'YES!' he threw his arm straight up in the air. 'A joke!'

What do you get from nervous cows?

Milk shakes!

He took the first lolly stick upstairs and put it in an empty shoe-box.

'Yes, I'm pathetic,' he told Waffle dog. 'But I *am* going to win that colour telly.'

He folded his glasses onto the bedside table and was asleep almost before his head hit the pillow.

* * *

It seemed he'd only just closed his eyes.

'Are you going to stay there all day?' Mum shouted from the doorway. 'I'll be back around two. I'm dropping Lucy off at the child minder's. Now behave yourself.'

Albie grunted and crawled back under the

covers. Then suddenly he jerked himself up. 'Where's that other lolly stick?'

He leaped out of bed and pulled on his clothes in record time. In a second, trainers flapping open, he was wandering outside staring down at the gutter.

'What are you doing?' Tash Ferris shouted out as she walked towards him with a carton of milk in her hand. 'Lost some money?'

'Oh . . . er, yeah. Twenty pence fell out of my pocket!'

Tash looked him up and down carefully. 'What pocket?'

Albie patted his shorts, desperately searching for a pocket shape. There wasn't one. 'Ha ha!' he laughed a fake laugh. 'I lost it yesterday. Yesterday evening, silly me!'

Tash raised her eyes to heaven. 'For a minute,' she pointed at a lolly stick lying in the gutter just behind him, 'I thought you were looking for that!'

'Who, me?' Albie was horrified. 'No, I was looking for . . .'

'Then you won't mind me having it?' Tash bent down and picked up the lolly stick. 'Have you heard this one? *What crisps fly?*' She burst out laughing. 'Eeeek, eeek, eeeeeeek.'

'Salt and Winger?'

'No!' Tash creased up. '**Plain ones**, silly.'

'That's rubbish!' Albie scoffed. He began to wish he hadn't invited her into his house. She only knew about the competition because of him and her family probably had a colour television in their house already.

'Well, must be off. Mum's waiting for her cup of tea.' Tash waved the carton of milk at him and pushed the lolly stick down her pocket. 'Maybe see you later!' she teased.

'I doubt it,' Albie said, deciding not to allow her to make a fool of him. 'Don't think I fancy you!' he muttered under his breath. 'Not in a million years would I ask you out!'

Girls! They were a waste of time and energy! He was deep in thought when he trod on one of the very things he was searching for. He picked up the stick and unfolded it to read the joke.

What's Santa Claus's wife called?

Mary Christmas.

'Yeah, right,' Albie shoved the stick down his sock for now.

Then he looked up and saw revolting Big Malco. He'd spotted him once before on the last day of term and decided to keep away from him at all costs. Big Malco was bigger and more scary than any boy he'd ever seen. And when he spoke he sounded about a hundred years old. It was hard to believe he was still in Middle School.

Albie ducked through the park hedge hoping Big Malco hadn't seen him. He had just picked up a rolled up plastic bag from under a park bench when Big Malco caught up with him.

'You're the new kid. Where do you live?'

'France,' Albie said, not wanting to tell him.

'Yeah, sure!' Big Malco sneered. 'Disneyland, by any chance?'

'Rome!' Albie said. 'Know it?'

Big Malco looked at him as if he was crazy. 'Rome's not in France,' he said slowly. 'Are you stupid?'

'Who, me?' said Albie, quickly. 'Of course Rome's not in France. Who said it was?'

Big Malco was lost for a second. 'Er . . .' Then he began staring at the plastic bag in Albie's hand. 'What's that for?'

'Just . . .' Albie couldn't come up with a reason for having a crumpled old plastic bag in his hand. 'Things . . .'

'Things, eh? What things?' Big Malco said in that sulky way of his. 'Well, mate?'

'Yep, things. You know, bits and pieces. This

24

and that,' Albie said, praying for a sewer to open up in front of him. Suddenly a way out came into his head in the form of a question. 'Anything interesting to do round here?'

It worked. 'Got a bike?' Big Malco said.

'No,' Albie looked away. This could still go badly. One wrong move and he was liable to end up as a fence post. 'I'm getting a new bike soon, though. I've outgrown my old one which was a twenty-four gear job,' he lied.

'Really?' Big Malco said, dismissing the lie. 'In that case, there isn't anything to do round here unless you want to spend your time stuffing lolly sticks down your socks!'

He stared at Albie's scribble of a sock with a lolly stick poking out, then slowly eyed the crumpled plastic bag again. 'You've got a problem! Do you know that?'

'Yeah, of course,' Albie looked up at the sky and wished a huge meteorite would blast Big Malco away. 'That's what the doctor told me. He said it was either that or I was a genius! You know how it is . . .' Albie was saying anything to play for time. 'Sometimes you see a plastic bag all crumpled up and you think, why didn't someone put that in the bin? I mean, what's the point of leaving it there? It's just . . .'

At that moment, another tall boy he recognized from school shouted: 'What you talking to the new kid for, Malco? He's a worm.'

Albie stepped back on the grass as Dopes Holroyd kicked the hedge and tried to push Big Malco into it. Dopes Holroyd fancied himself. It was obvious by the looks he gave everyone. But right now, Albie was very pleased to see him. Dopes wasn't quite as effective as a meteorite but he would do in an emergency.

'Call me a worm? You idiot!' Albie thought. 'Who do you think you are?'

'Wanna come swimming?' Dopes asked Big Malco, ignoring Albie, who was busy walking backwards away from them.

'Might as well,' Big Malco pretended to strangle his friend as they climbed over the hedge. 'There's nothing going on round here.'

Albie breathed out. They'd gone. That's the

way it happened sometimes. One minute you were talking to someone and about to become minced cheese and the next minute he'd walked off and forgotten all about you. It was as if you'd suddenly become invisible. In this case, it was just as well. Big Malco was no joke.

Albie plucked the lolly stick from his sock and put it in the plastic bag. Nine hundred and ninety-eight to go.

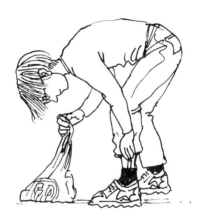

CHAPTER 3

Dangling

Late that afternoon, wandering around picking up sticks, Albie found himself the other side of Heveling, walking past all the units on the Industrial Estate. Something made him look up at the building opposite.

'Wait a minute!' A bright yellow sign, dripping with neon cornets seemed to stare back at him. It said: Hill's Ice-cream Unit! 'This is fate!' Albie decided with amazement.

'Maybe this will do it!' he said quietly as he wandered across the road trying to look innocent and not like a kid about to steal hundreds of lolly sticks. Being Sunday, there wasn't a soul around. After looking up and down once more to check the street was empty, Albie tied the plastic bag securely to his arm and dived at the brick wall as if it were an upright swimming pool.

'Yah!' he screamed as his foot caught hold and he hauled himself up the bricks to the top. It occurred to him that he might have gone stone mad as he looked all the way down to the street below, but then he climbed over the top of the wall in one quick move.

He bounced on to the concrete on the other side. The first thing he saw was two white Hill's Ice-cream vans parked next to the unit entrance. Just as he picked out four black bins lined up beside them, he also spied a fierce black dog twitching a wet nose at him from the corner of the building.

'Oh, oh!' Albie turned and dived back up the bricks. Maybe this wasn't such a good idea. He tried to climb back up the wall but couldn't

make his arms reach high enough to get far. He was shaking too much.

'Grrrr!' The black dog scrabbled at his dangling knees. One last heave. Albie dug his fingernails in, swallowed air until his head swam and let out a huge 'Yah!' as his elbows lifted into the air and he scooted up the wall and swung himself over, the blood thumping wildly in his ears. 'Yes!'

The black dog tried to climb the wall after him, barking madly.

Albie fell in a heap on the ground. He bounced back against the wall and shivered. Hunched over, he waited for his breathing to come back to normal again.

It was getting late. Mum would be wondering where on earth he was. He looked back at the grey building and sighed with relief. He couldn't think now why he'd had the stupid idea of climbing over the wall to search the bins for lolly sticks.

'Got anything?' Suddenly a huge figure emerged from the shadows. Albie was too puffed to answer. 'What did you get in there?'

The voice sounded so terrifying Albie hardly recognized it. 'Nothing! I haven't got nothing!'

'No?' Big Malco emerged sulkily from the alley and Albie was glad it was only him and not an axe murderer. 'You've still got that plastic bag, mate. What's your problem?'

'I, I . . .' Albie was too weak with relief to answer.

Big Malco walked towards him. 'What's in that thing?' He grabbed the bag from Albie's wrist. 'Let's see.' He tore the bag open and fingered the dirty lolly sticks with jokes that Albie had taken over the wall and back again. 'You really ought to see someone about this, mate!'

Albie agreed. 'Yeah, I know, but I just can't

seem to stop. Something comes over me and I go all weird and have to collect things.' He fiddled with a snag in his jeans, 'Some days I get it worse than others. Once I was . . .'

'Shut up, mate!' Big Malco said. Albie stopped in his tracks. He waited for Big Malco's fist to land in his mouth. 'We'd have better luck over there.' Big Malco pointed at the next building, Casey's Computer Services. 'There's loads of stuff to nick.'

'I've got to get back.' Albie hoped his voice sounded stronger than it felt. 'Had enough for today!'

'All right then, we'll do it tomorrow!' Big Malco smiled. 'Okay, mate?' Albie shuddered. He'd never stolen anything in his life. Well, apart from that plastic knight he'd taken from nursery school when he was about three. His mum had made him take it back. She would kill him if she'd seen him climbing over that wall.

Now he was stuck. He couldn't admit to Big Malco what he'd actually been doing. Big Malco would make him the joke of the neighbourhood.

'Never mind, mate!' Big Malco put an arm round his shoulder. He felt sorry for him. 'Where you off to now then?' he asked.

'Home!' Albie said, twitching his shoulders as if he was suffering from some tic or other. He turned and headed off towards the main road.

'I'll walk with you,' Big Malco pushed his hands down his pockets and strode along beside him. Albie groaned inside.

'Where else have you done?' Big Malco asked, as they crossed the road. A shiver ran down Albie's back. A lorry thundered past too loud for Albie to answer. 'I remember the first job I did,' Big Malco went on. 'It was the school office when I was six. The secretary left me in there while she went off somewhere and I just opened the drawer. Stole a calculator and some note pads. I was dead pleased. My mum thought it was hilarious. Told me to take the computer next time.'

Albie swallowed hard, a joke about mummies came to mind.

Why was the Egyptian boy worried?

Because his daddy was a mummy!

It made him feel better and he started to laugh. Big Malco seemed to think Albie was laughing because of what he was telling him and went on talking about all the things he'd nicked in his life. By the time they got to 23 Churchill Road, Albie felt as sick as a dog. He'd even forgotten he hadn't wanted Big Malco to know where he lived.

'See you,' Albie ran up the short path to his house without looking back.

'Yeah, 'bye, mate!' Big Malco called after him.

Mate . . . He'd kept calling him mate. It was getting on his nerves.

* * *

'Eat your tea. Lucy's finished hers!' Mum plonked the fish fingers and chips on the table.

'Nellie hasn't finished!' Lucy grinned, pushing her pony's head into the tomato ketchup.

'Do you know there's a fun music afternoon at the playing fields tomorrow?' Mum said.

Albie shook his head. He could feel his heart still thumping. Lucy stamped her white pony's foot in his fish finger making a large hole. Then she stuck her pink pony's nose in a chip, flattening it.

'Mum, tell her!' Albie pulled his plate away. 'She's mashing up my tea.'

'Lucy!' Mum said. 'Stop it!'

'Nellie's hungry,' Lucy screamed.

'Too bad!' Albie pushed the pink pony off his plate. 'So am I.'

Lucy wiped the pony's eyes with her sleeve. 'There, there, don't cry! He didn't mean to shout at you.'

'I did!' Albie said crossly.

'Now, now,' Mum sighed. 'The music thing's been organized for local kids,' she went on. 'I suppose the council feels guilty it doesn't have a youth club. Tash came over earlier and wondered if you'd like to go. She's got some free tickets!'

'Dunno,' Albie said, feeling sorry for himself.

'Bet it's awful, but what else is there to do?' Suddenly he remembered that Big Malco had something for him to do. 'Yeah, I'd love to go. That'll be great. Fantastic. I'll go and see Tash after tea.'

Mum was a bit taken back by his enthusiasm. 'Maybe you should dig out your clarinet and get up on the stage with them!' This was going too far.

'No way!' Albie hadn't looked at his clarinet for two years and he'd forgotten how to play the high notes. 'I never even liked the clarinet. You made me play it because Gran used to play it. I didn't even want her to give it to me.'

'But you were so good at it,' Mum sighed. 'You should have kept it up.'

'Nellie likes playing cladiret, don't you?' Lucy started neighing loudly. 'You can give cladiret to her.'

'Clarinet!' Albie corrected her and got up from the table. He'd had enough. His tea was nothing but mashed-up slosh. He was having to go out with Tash, who didn't even like him, in order to avoid Big Malco who thought he was a burglar. And now Mum was going to make him play the clarinet again. All because he had decided to enter a competition for a colour television set. Life!

CHAPTER 4

Lemon and lime

How does a monster count up to ten?

On his fingers!

'Ha, ha. Thirty-four all together,' Albie sat on his bed counting. 'Only . . .' He tried to work out how many more he needed to get. 'Four from ten is six. Hang on . . . thirty from a hundred is seventy. Take away . . . That's nine hundred and . . . IMPOSSIBLE!' he shouted, stomping down the stairs and out of the house to Tash's.

He lifted the polished brass door knocker to the highest limit and let it drop with a thud. He heard footsteps padding down the hall. The door opened a fraction.

'Hi,' Tash said, poking her nose out.

'*Knock, knock!*' Albie said.

'*Who's there?*' Tash sighed.

'*Dishes.*'

'*Dishes who?*'

'*Dishes me*,' Albie smiled. 'Hello!'

'Who is it?' a woman's voice called from the back of the house.

'A friend,' Tash shouted back down the hallway.

'Who, dear?' the voice demanded. 'Who is it?'

'No one you know, Mum,' Tash said crossly. 'A friend of mine.' She looked at Albie, who was surprised to hear she considered him a friend. Maybe she was lonely?

'Not many people come round,' Tash explained. 'Only social services. You know how it is.' Albie nodded, not having a clue what she was talking about. 'Come in, then.' She opened the door wide and Albie noticed she'd pushed her black, tangly hair behind her ears. She looked pretty in that little blue T-shirt. She flashed her wriggling tadpole eyes at him, making him go all nervous, and led him into the lounge.

'Who are you?' Tash's mum looked shocked to see a boy standing before her.

'Er . . . Albie Tilek.' Albie shuffled about uncomfortably. 'I live um . . .'

'In the street, Mum. They're the new people I told you about.'

'Well, don't stay too long. Tash's got more than enough to do!' her mum said, turning the wheelchair back towards the large, wide screen, television set with three loudspeakers and a matching video, in the corner of the room.

'Sorry,' Albie said as they headed into the

small kitchen where a portable television stood next to the fridge. 'I didn't know . . .'

'It's okay. Well, most of the time it's okay. I've been her primary carer for two years now. I'm getting used to it. Though sometimes I wish I had a sister or a brother or someone to help. Dad's very good but he's at work most of the time, so it's mostly down to me.' Albie smiled at her.

'You can have Lucy to help any time you want!' he offered. Tash was very pretty he suddenly decided. 'Lucy's good at answering the telephone. Well, actually her ponies are good at answering the . . .'

'Thanks,' Tash said. 'But, no thanks.'

'I don't mind you collecting lolly sticks as well,' he said kindly, hoping he wouldn't regret it later.

She threw back her head and laughed. 'Eeeeeeek, eek, eek. It took you a long time to say that, didn't it?'

Albie had to admit she was right, it had. 'I suppose so,' he shook his head. 'By the way, do you know Big Malco?'

'Him? He's trouble. Don't have anything to do with him,' she warned.

'I wasn't going to.' Albie vowed never to speak to him again no matter what. 'I just wondered if you knew him.'

'Everyone knows him!' Then she changed the subject. 'You coming to the music thingy tomorrow?'

'Sure,' Albie smiled. 'Might as well.' He didn't have the nerve to ask why she was inviting him.

'It starts at three. Come round at half-past two. The weather man says it's going to be boiling hot tomorrow and Hill's Ice-cream are always there. Last year they had four vans out. We can collect loads of sticks.'

Just then Albie had a horrible vision of Tash being presented with a colour television set for her bedroom. He'd already seen the fantastic telly in the lounge and the portable telly in the kitchen looked brand new.

'There are four first prizes you know,' Tash said, folding her arms. 'We both might be winners.'

'Yeah and pigs might fly,' Albie sniffed. Why did she want another television set? 'They won't give two prizes to people living in the same street. It'll look fixed.'

'You don't know that,' Tash said.

'Sweetie,' her mum called out. 'I could do with that cocoa you promised to make.'

'I'm doing it,' Tash grabbed the kettle and pushed the switch down.

'Better go,' Albie smiled. 'See you tomorrow.'

'Right, 'bye.' Tash flashed her wriggling tadpole eyes at him for longer than usual. He wondered again if she fancied him. She showed him out.

'Nah,' Albie said to himself as he walked up his path pushing his glasses back up his nose. 'No one's ever fancied me.'

* * *

All of a sudden an ice-cream van sounded its silly horn and turned the corner into his street.

It was a Hill's Ice-cream van.

'Can I have a lolly, Mum?' Albie ran into the lounge. 'Please!'

'Go on, take the money from my purse and get me a strawberry split. What do you want Lucy?'

'Er . . . I'll have a . . . no, er . . .' She tapped her cheek with her finger to help her think.

'Hurry up,' Albie said crossly, taking some change from Mum's purse. 'He'll be gone by the time you decide.'

'A . . . a . . .' Lucy tried to think. 'You,' she kissed a silver pony on his bottom, 'want ice-creamy?'

'That's it. You can have what I get you,' Albie ran out of the door.

'Cornet wiv chocolate log,' Lucy shouted after he'd gone.

Two minutes later, Albie was back with three lollies.

'Where's my cornet?' Lucy wailed. 'Mum, where's pony's ice-creamy?'

'Never mind,' Mum said.

'I didn't hear you,' Albie handed her the lemon and lime lolly. 'You had one of these last time.'

'No!' Lucy screwed up her face and stamped the floor. 'Pony hates lolly.'

She threw the lolly across the room where it landed on the sofa and stomped off upstairs, silver pony under her arm.

'Take it up to her,' Mum said, sucking her strawberry split. Albie grabbed the lemon and lime lolly from the sofa before Waffle got there and ran upstairs eating his banana lolly, which tasted like custard.

'Here,' Albie said. 'It's lemon and lime.'

Lucy turned her face to the wall. 'Won't!'

'I'll have it then!' Albie said, pulling off the wrapper.

Lucy turned round angrily and stabbed the silver pony at him. 'Give pony his lolly!' she said. 'Now, you pig.'

Albie handed it over and watched her lick the lemon and lime right down to the last dribble. He sucked the end of his lolly and read the joke:

Where do ghosts go swimming?

In the Dead Sea!

He collected Lucy's stick from the floor:

Why did the car have a puncture?

There was a fork in the road!

Albie grabbed Mum's stick before she broke it up into splinters:

What do dinosaurs eat for dinner?

Jurassic pork!

He now had thirty-seven. He calculated it would take about a year to collect a thousand sticks at this

rate, and there were only two days left. He might as well give up.

* * *

'I found your clarinet by the way.' Mum handed him the music case. 'It's such a beautiful thing, why don't you clean it and have a little practice?'

And because Albie had nothing else to do, no television to watch, no new magazine to read, he took the clarinet case up to his bedroom, took the pieces out and carefully put them together.

Then he stood in front of the mirror, swished his brown hair from side to side and curled his top lip.

'This is for all those saddos who are collecting lolly sticks,' Albie snarled. 'Huh, I mean *you*.' And he pointed the clarinet at his own reflection. 'Come on, now!'

'*Lolly woe!*' he sang and blew a perfect note. He took a deep breath, threw his head back and flared his nostrils. '*Ohhhh, Lolly woe. It really has to go, has to go, has to go,*' he sang as loud as he could.

Suddenly he stopped for a second and looked
at himself. Words formed in his mouth:

'You and me babe working hard all day
Need those flavours in our nose
like a stone between our toes.'

He shook his glasses all over his face and played a long line of mad notes that came out like a scream:

'Cause babe we've got . . .

Those lolly, lolly woes,

Ohhhh, lolly woe. It really has to go, has to go, has to go.'

'Cor!' Lucy stood with her mouth open at the door. 'Nellie liked that!'

Mum soon arrived. 'Albie, that was great! I'd forgotten how well you could play.'

'I just made it up,' Albie said, surprised at the fantastic song that seemed to write itself as soon as he put the clarinet between his lips. 'Not bad, eh?' he looked down his nose at his audience.

'Your glasses are falling off,' Mum said and brought him back to Heveling.

CHAPTER 5

Danger point!

'They have to be in tomorrow,' Albie said. 'If I don't collect hundreds of lolly sticks today, I've had it!'

'And me!' Tash said as they strolled along the road the next afternoon, staring at the pavement.

'Got one,' Albie picked up a bent lolly stick from the gutter. '*Which fish can only be seen at night?*'

'Let me see,' Tash sighed. 'Yep, ***a starfish***.'

Albie nodded. 'Why didn't you laugh?'

'Because,' Tash shrugged, 'it's not that funny.'

'Right,' Albie agreed. 'So tell me your funniest joke!'

'*If buttercups are yellow,*' Tash said, '*what colour are hiccups?*'

Albie bit his bottom lip. 'Sickup blue?'

'Eeek, eeeek, eeeeek,' Tash laughed so much she could hardly say it. '**Burple!** Eeek, eeek.'

'Ha, ha, ha,' Albie said, trying to laugh a bit harder. 'Ha! Yeah, that's really good.'

They walked on towards the playing fields. 'Do you think they will allow bent sticks with chewed ends?' Albie plucked a doubled-up stick from the hedge.

'No,' Tash said.

'Do you ever think about the blobs of invisible spit on these things?' Albie pretended to throw up on the grass. 'Ugh!'

'Why would I do that? Tash said. 'It would only make me feel ill. Anyway I only touch the ends, just in case.'

'Yeah, but you don't know which end you're touching,' Albie said. 'It could be the end which has been licked by someone's smelly tongue.'

'Shut up!' Tash yelled. 'You missed this one.' She grabbed a lolly stick from the top of an open bin. *'Can an elephant jump higher than a tree?'*

'Yes!' Albie guessed.

'No!' She waved the stick in the air like an Oscar. ***'Trees can't jump, stupid.'***

'Good one!' Albie laughed. 'Hang on,' he shouted, racing after her. 'You've got the plastic bags.'

Tash slowed down, pulled two white bags from her pocket and handed one to him. 'May the best collector win,' she said.

'Me, you mean!' Albie grinned, uncurling the bag to put the lolly sticks in. 'You don't stand a chance!'

'Hey!' Albie turned to see Big Malco standing beside him. How did he always manage to appear out of thin air, Albie wondered? 'What is it with you and plastic bags, mate?' Big Malco asked.

'I er . . .' Albie turned pale. He didn't need this.

'He's cleaning up the neighbourhood,' Tash said. 'Want to help?'

'Yeah, right!' Big Malco gave her a sulky smile, 'As if. Why aren't you at home, Nurse Ferris, looking after your mum?'

'Because this is my day off,' Tash scowled back. 'Why aren't you in prison?'

'I've just escaped.' Big Malco made a Frankenstein face. 'Are you frightened?'

'Ha! Of you? You're as scary as Swiss cheese.' She turned to Albie, *'How do you make a Swiss roll?'*

Albie shook his head. 'Don't know.'

*'**Push him off an Alp.**'* Tash turned and walked off. 'See you later,' she called to Albie.

Big Malco raised his fist to her back. 'Why are you hanging round with Nurse Ferris?' he said. 'She's no fun. You should catch sight of Natalie Granger. She's really gorgeous. You've never seen anyone like her. Whoar! She might even be here this afternoon with a bit of luck. I'll introduce you to her if you like, mate.'

'Yeah, great,' Albie said, trying to sound keen.

'Thanks a lot.'

'Are we on for later?' Big Malco asked. 'Casey's Computer place, remember?'

'Er . . .' Albie fiddled with his plastic bag. 'No, I have to babysit Lucy.'

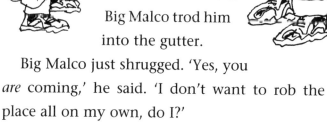

'Bring her with you,' Big Malco said. 'I don't mind. She can be lookout,' he suggested.

'No way!' Albie stared at him. 'And I'm not coming!' He was surprised how easy it had been to say no and now he didn't even care if Big Malco trod him into the gutter.

Big Malco just shrugged. 'Yes, you *are* coming,' he said. 'I don't want to rob the place all on my own, do I?'

Just then, a crowd of boys crossed the road and waved at Big Malco. Everyone seemed to be a friend of his. 'See you around six,' Big Malco tapped Albie on the shoulder. 'I'll find you wherever you are, mate!'

Albie gritted his teeth. How was he going to get out of this? Then he remembered the music afternoon didn't end until seven. If he could hang around with Tash until the last moment he might be able to avoid a life of crime. It was worth a chance.

But where had Tash gone?

* * *

Before he found her, ten minutes later, he'd collected thirteen more lolly sticks.

'How many have you got?' Tash shouted from the middle of the playing fields. Albie screwed up his eyes. All he could really see was the bulky plastic bag she was waving at him.

'Fourteen!' he called back. 'You?'

'Not telling,' she screamed and burst out

laughing. 'Eeek, eek, eeeeek! *What country has no fat people?* **Finland!**' she shouted before he could answer. He had two of those.

'Right!' Albie decided. 'I'm going to beat her.'

Instead of walking towards her he turned and ran the other way. The field was filling up with people. Hundreds of kids everywhere. Families sitting on the grass waiting for the music to begin.

Albie ran right up to a Hill's Ice-cream van parked at the edge of the playing fields. The sun came out. A long queue formed. Albie collected every lolly stick in sight. 'Seventy-three!' he said after half an hour. 'This is easy!'

Now and then a kid from school recognized him and looked him up and down as if he was a maniac. Albie just went on whistling to himself and scrabbling in the grass and under trees for sticks. No doubt he was going to get a reputation after this event. 'Yeah, he's that mad kid who cleans up all the time.' But he didn't care. For the moment things were going well and he wasn't going to be beaten by a girl. No way!

* * *

He wiped sticky toffee from two sticks on to his jeans; cleaned lumpy bits from others on to tree bark; smeared the grass with orange, blue and green dribble from a whole bunch of sticks, and carefully examined red marks at the edge of the sticks to see whether the colour was lipstick or blood.

He couldn't relax for a second. There were broken and twisted sticks to be straightened, sticks without jokes to throw in the bin. And all those smelly sticks dipped in brown ketchup and smelling of onion to put away as fast as possible. It was a revolting job all right. A band started playing. Albie didn't even bother to look across the field at the stage.

* * *

The ice-cream van sold out and drove off. The sun beat down. Albie sat on a bank and closed his aching eyes for a while. All that looking for sticks had made him tired.

He made a pillow of his hot hands and carefully placed the two full bags of lolly sticks by his side. Then he drifted off to the sound of distant drums.

There he was in the *Heveling Weekly News*. Front page. A massive photo of a smiling, handsome Albie being presented with a huge colour television set from Hill's Ice-cream. Standing next to him was a clapping, adoring Tash Ferris and also Natalie Granger, who looked remarkably like a Hollywood actress. *'Man of the Week,'* the headline said.

'Wow, he's great!' Natalie Granger whispered to Tash.

'Yeah,' Tash sighed. 'Isn't he?'

'You can't have him, he's mine!' Natalie Granger hissed.

'No, he isn't,' Tash pushed her over. 'I saw him first.' They started to fight.

'Hey, girls,' Albie turned around. 'That's enough.'

Suddenly something kicked him in the side. He jerked up in pain. 'Ow!' he opened his eyes.

'You're hopeless.' Tash stood in front of him. 'I bet you haven't even got a hundred sticks yet.'

Albie was disappointed to see Tash's cross face staring at him instead of her adoring face in his dreams. 'Come on! You can't lie around all day.'

'I only sat down for a second,' Albie said, noticing the sun was much lower in the sky. He jumped up and followed her wearily to a black bin.

'Hey,' he yelled. 'This is my patch.'

'I don't see your name anywhere,' Tash

laughed pulling sticky sticks and a banana skin from the bin. *'How do you make a banana split?'*

'I know that one!' Albie caught up with her.

*'**Cut it in half**,'* Tash said.

'I told you I knew it. They're mine.' Albie tried to grab the sticks. 'Let go!' he warned, clenching her wrist.

'What is it with you?' Tash tightened her grip on the sticks.

Albie let go. 'Sorry,' he said, suddenly realizing he was getting a bit too desperate. 'I didn't mean to . . .'

'Here,' she handed him the sticks. 'Have them all if you're so scared I'll win.' She dropped her full plastic bag on the grass. 'And this!' She slapped a banana skin on his shoulder and walked off in a temper, flicking her tangly hair as she walked.

'Hey,' Albie shouted after her. 'Why are you always walking off? I didn't do anything. I wasn't . . .'

Girls! They were impossible to understand. Albie decided not to waste any more time wondering what Tash was up to. This was war, with a huge colour television at stake and only one day left. He didn't have time to worry about what she might be thinking.

He picked her bag up from the grass and made a hole at the top so he would know which one was hers. Then he tied the plastic bags together and looped them through his arms. They banged against his knees every time he moved. Eyes down, shoulders hunched, Albie walked round the field step by step, collecting every stick in his path.

* * *

Albie worked on across the field and when he finally looked up he found himself at the side of the stage.

'And now,' the compere said in a husky voice into the microphone, 'it's time for you out there to take part. The stage is empty and full of musical instruments. Who wants to come up and play a solo for us?' Albie looked at all the kids sitting on the grass. Only one toddler showed any interest in getting on stage and his mother yanked him back before he could bang the drum with his rattle. Albie slowly untangled a piece of string from a stick.

'Come on, someone!' the compere begged. 'Please!' A baby in the front row threw a dummy at him and just missed the microphone. Everyone laughed.

'Pheep,' a deafening whistle made Albie screw up his eyes. Big Malco waved wildly as he made his way through the crowd towards him.

'Oh, no!' Albie leaped onto the stage, heart thumping.

'Yes, we have a player, everyone,' the compere smiled at him. The audience clapped. 'Over here, boy. What instrument do you play?' Albie gazed around him in terror. Big Malco stood in front of him on the grass and gave him a look that said, 'I'm waiting!'

'Clarinet,' Albie said without thinking, all the while desperately searching for some way of ducking out.

'Here you are.' The compere took a clarinet from a box and handed it to him. 'What's your name, son?'

Albie dropped his bags of lolly sticks. 'Albie Tilek,' he said.

'Let's all welcome Albie Tilek,' the relieved compere started clapping. The crowd whistled and shouted. Albie looked out at a sea of strange, smiling faces. In the middle, Big Malco was scratching his chin, watching his every move.

Albie put the clarinet to his mouth. He licked his lips. His heart thudded. A camera flash went off in his face and made him blink.

'*Oh, lolly woe,*' he sang out as if it was a proper song. Then he played a mad melody, totally unlike the one he'd sung to his bedroom mirror. '*It really has to go, has to go, has to go,*' he sang louder, before blowing some As.

'*You and me babe working hard all day.*' Then he added an '*ooooh*' before going on:

'*Need those flavours in our nose*
Like a stone between our toes.

'*Cause babe we've got . . .*' he parped out a long line of complicated notes that surprised even himself. The crowd went wild. Out of the corner of his eyes Albie noticed the surprised look on the compere's face. It seemed to say, 'That's good.'

Albie screeched: *'Hey babe!'* and sang on:

'Those lolly, lolly woes,

Ohhhh, lolly woe. It really has to go, has to go, has to go,' and followed with loads of F minors and B flats. 'Peeeep-peep!'

The crowd roared, 'More!'

Albie felt like a real jazz player. He closed his eyes, took a deep breath and played Lolly Woe again. Only this time he played it the way he thought a jazz player would. He added lots more notes and swayed the clarinet around like he'd seen in a film.

When he got to the chorus he shook his brown hair from side to side and kicked his knee up. The crowd went mad. They didn't seem to notice that the tune was different this time.

His glasses fell down his nose and he left them hanging there. One or two kids stamped their feet. The front row stood up. Three girls linked arms and swayed. Albie grinned at them. It was unbelievable.

The compere clapped and clapped, at the same time warning him with his eyes to hurry up and finish. Cameras flashed in Albie's eyes.

He decided to sing the song again and played a note so high it reached danger point.

CHAPTER 6

The plastic bag boy

'Thank you, Albie Tilek,' the compere suddenly reached for the clarinet and brought him down to earth. Albie tried to pull the instrument back. He was just getting going. This was the most fun he'd had in ages.

'*Oh, baby,*' Albie wailed like someone on 'Top Of The Pops'. Two girls screamed.

'Don't push it!' the compere snarled at Albie and gave him a look that told him to get off the stage, now! But Albie couldn't be stopped.

'*It really has to go, has to go,*' he waved the

clarinet in the air. The compere tried to catch it. The crowd roared louder.

The compere grabbed Albie by the shoulders and hauled him to the side of the stage. 'You're only supposed to have five minutes, you know.' Albie didn't care. He just grinned sideways at the maze of faces watching his every move.

As he waved goodbye to his screaming fans, he spotted Big Malco out of the corner of his eye striding towards him. Albie grabbed the plastic bags as if they were full of gold, jumped off the stage and ran as fast as he could, chased closely by three very young girls waving autograph books and pencils. So this was fame!

'We want Albie,' the smallest one screamed. The other two joined in, 'We want Albie! We want Albie.' The shouting got louder. 'Albie, Albie, wait for us!'

'Go away!' Albie shouted back and dived behind an oak tree. Big Malco was doubled up, laughing his head off.

Albie peered out. The girls caught up with him. 'Oooh,' they squealed. 'Give us your autograph!' Albie quickly signed his name and ran off to the edge of the field, through the nettles and out of sight from everyone. This was unreal. He stopped for a minute to get his breath back. What now?

* * *

Albie ran home, dumped his bag of lolly sticks on the bed, closed the door tight so Waffle couldn't get in and eat them all and ran off to Tash's house with her bag of sticks.

He decided not to go home again until much later. Until there was no chance of finding Big Malco waiting for him outside. He lifted the knocker to the highest limit then let it drop with a thud.

Tash poked her nose round the door. 'Oh, it's you,' she said.

'Can I come in? Big Malco's looking for me.'

Tash opened the door wide and he stepped into the hall. 'Why is he looking for you?'

'Dunno!' Albie shrugged.

Tash didn't smile at him. She was cross all right.

'What's up?' Albie asked.

'Nothing, why?'

'No?' Albie raised his eyebrows. 'You sure?' She was the moodiest person he'd ever met. 'Here's your bag of sticks, by the way!'

'Thanks.' Tash took the plastic bag from him as if she didn't care whether she had them back or not.

'I made a small hole at the top of the bag, so I'd know which one was yours,' Albie tried to show her how nice he was, but she ignored him.

He followed her down the hall to the kitchen, where on a stool in front of him sat the most gorgeous girl Albie had ever seen in his life.

'Hi!' the vision smiled at him. Albie nodded at her. He couldn't speak. Tash looked at his face and almost snarled: 'Natalie Granger, Albie Tilek.'

'Hi, Albie, saw you playing the clarinet.' The vision twisted a length of blonde hair into a rope at the side of her face. 'I used to play the flute, but I was hopeless at it. You were great.'

'Thanks,' was all he managed to say after the best compliment he'd ever had in the whole of his life.

Tash folded her arms and looked from one to the other in a fury. 'It wasn't that great!' she said.

'No?' Natalie smiled at her and then him. Albie stared at his shoes. He wasn't used to this amount of attention from girls. It was as if his fantasy was coming true. Any minute he would have to stop them fighting over him. He couldn't help smiling.

Tash curled her lips. 'So you're off now?' she said to Natalie.

'Right.' Natalie quickly understood that she wasn't wanted. 'Better get going.' She slid off the stool. "Bye Tash,' she gave her friend a sweet smile. 'Oh, and I see what you mean.' They gave each other a knowing look that baffled Albie. Natalie twisted another length of hair into a rope, and let it go suddenly so it swished all over her shoulder as she walked out of the door.

'So you fancy her?' Tash said as soon as Natalie had gone. 'Everyone does.'

'Who, me?' Albie said. 'Nah!' He looked at the clock. It was a quarter-past six. Big Malco might still be waiting for him.

Tash stared out of the window, arms crossed.

'She's not bad,' Albie gulped. 'But she's not my type. I'm not into blondes.' He remembered an actor had said that once in a film.

Tash unfolded her arms and gave him the nicest smile in the world. 'Really, you did play the clarinet well. But I didn't want to say it then,' she said. 'It's just that . . . you know . . .'

It occurred to Albie that she was behaving as if she fancied him. He should say something, but what? 'Er . . .' he started. 'I um . . .'

Tash waited so long for him to speak, she

started to sigh. In the end, all he could come up with was: 'How many lolly sticks have you got?'

'That's for me to know,' she said. 'I haven't counted the ones from today. Thanks for bringing them back, by the way. How many have you got?'

'Hundreds,' Albie grinned. 'I'm going back down there in a minute to clear up the rest. Coming?'

Tash bit her bottom lip. 'Well . . .'

'Come on,' Albie tried again. 'We haven't done the other side of the field!' He felt pathetic! She tapped her foot, not quite sure. Albie stared at her. That wasn't what he'd meant to say. Why couldn't he ask her out or something?

'MUM,' Tash shouted down the hall. 'I'm going out for half an hour.' She grabbed a pile of empty plastic bags and pulled Albie towards the door.

'No!' her mother called after them. 'I need you to . . .' But the front door slammed shut before she finished.

Albie looked up and down the street. It was

clear. No Big Malco anywhere. They wandered back to the playing fields in silence and picked up lolly sticks for what seemed like hours.

'There's a pile over here,' Albie or Tash would shout from time to time. The field was still full of people. Some were lying on the grass. Some were slowly making their way home. The stage was being taken down. The last ice-cream van was packing up. Everywhere there was a smell of hot dogs and chips. Albie kept treading on empty crisp packets. It made him feel hungry.

'*When are eyes not eyes?*' Albie shouted. 'Know it?'

'No idea!' Tash laughed.

'***When they water.***' Albie straightened up. His back ached. His eyes hurt. A policeman with hair the colour of egg yolk walked towards him. Albie smiled at him. The policeman frowned. 'You're the plastic bag boy,' the policeman said, as if it was a joke.

'What?' Albie said.

'You fit the description.' The policeman looked him up and down. 'What's your name?'

'Albie Tilek,' Albie said quickly, his heart racing.

'You better come with me, lad.'

'Why?' Albie was scared stiff. 'What did I do?' He gave Tash a pleading look.

'He's been with me all day, officer,' Tash said. 'What's he done?'

'Come along both of you. I just want to ask you a few questions. It won't take long.' The policeman nodded to the small police station on the other side of the main road. 'This way.'

Albie's heart sank. Maybe someone had seen him climbing over Hill's wall that day he began looking for lolly sticks. But there hadn't been anyone around. No one but . . . Big Malco. Yes, Big Malco. Why had the policeman called him the plastic bag boy? No one noticed he always had a plastic bag with him except for Big Malco.

This had something to do with him. He just knew it and the thought made him panic.

The policeman wrote down their names and addresses when they got to the police station and left them for a moment.

'My mum's on her own,' Tash worried. 'I can't sit here for hours.'

'Don't worry,' Albie said softly. 'I haven't done anything. They can't keep us here. It's against the law.'

'Okay,' the policeman opened the door. 'I've phoned your parents. No one at either of your homes.' He turned to Tash. 'When will your parents get back?'

'Not sure,' Tash lied. Why hadn't her mother answered the phone? The mobile was always on her lap. Something must have gone wrong. She could have hurt herself.

'I need to look in those bags!' the policeman took the plastic bags from their laps. He placed them on the table and opened each one. 'Lolly sticks?' he asked surprised.

'With jokes on,' Albie smiled. 'Not just

ordinary lolly sticks, as you can see!'

'Do you know a Derek Holroyd and a Malcolm Slater?' He looked from Albie to Tash. 'I'm Sergeant Austen, by the way.'

'Not really,' Tash said. 'They're criminals aren't they?'

'Do you mean Dopes Holroyd and Big Malco?' Albie said.

'Yes, I do, son,' Sergeant Austen nodded. 'It seems they've been picked up climbing over Casey's Computer Services' wall. Know anything about it?'

'We've been collecting lolly sticks all day!' Tash sighed. 'We're entering the competition at Hill's for a colour television set. Why would we know anything about what Big Malco and Dopes Holroyd have been up to?'

Albie agreed. 'Yeah, what's it got to do with us?'

'Well,' Sergeant Austen smiled. 'We've got Derek Holroyd and Malcolm Slater in the other room and they say you have all the stolen goods.'

'What?' Tash and Albie screamed at the same time.

'It's okay,' Sergeant Austen smiled. 'You can go now. It seems someone's been playing a joke on us!' Tash and Albie jumped up with their bags.

* * *

Tash couldn't get home quickly enough. She was worried sick about her mother. Albie could hardly keep up with her as she raced down

Churchill Road swinging her three bags full of lolly sticks all over the place.

'Want me to come in with you?' he shouted after her as she unlocked her front door. She shook her black, tangly hair and disappeared inside without answering. Albie stood on the street expecting her to appear again any second, but she didn't. Eventually he went home and climbed the stairs to his bedroom where he got the shock of his life!

CHAPTER 7

Eek, eek!

'LUCY, WHAT HAVE YOU DONE?' Albie screamed. He almost fainted at the sight in front of him. His chances of winning a colour telly were destroyed! Ruined!

Every surface was covered in damaged lolly sticks. All over the window-ledge lay piles of crushed and splintered lolly sticks. He almost trod on a huge, spiky ball of stick bits tied round an orange pony. The floor was covered in sticks twisted in half, broken in two. Some were tied with ribbons, arched round pony manes, decorated with transfers. It was horrible! And in the middle of it all, Waffle dog was stretched out on the bed, busy chewing his way through a heap of sticks as if they were fresh bones.

'LUCY!' Albie felt like crying.

'I'm just making stables,' Lucy stopped cracking a stick into the shape of a roof for a second and got up from the floor. 'Ponies like new stables!' She put a hand on her brother's arm. 'You can help me make some. I don't mind. There's lots more.'

* * *

Albie heard the front door bang downstairs.

'Yes, go up,' Mum said to Tash. She raced up the stairs two at a time.

'What the—?' Tash turned to stone when she saw what had happened. 'Oh, no!'

'I knew I wouldn't win a colour telly.' Albie sat down on the edge of the bed. He tried to stop his eyes watering. 'Right from the beginning, I had this feeling it wasn't meant to be.'

'Stop it,' Tash smiled. 'It's not the end of the world. We can rescue most of these. Come on!'

'What's the point?' Albie shook his head. 'I only had about six hundred anyway and now half of them are ruined! What chance have I got?'

'Hey, Lucy,' Tash turned to her. 'Sorry, but we need these sticks back!'

'It's okay,' Lucy said. 'These stables keep falling down and they smell. Nellie likes her sofa house better. Now she's been sick.' Lucy wiped the pink pony's mouth. 'Need a cuddly downstairs?' She kissed her mane and wandered off.

Albie fell back on the bed next to Waffle. 'I give up!'

'By the way, Mum's fine. She was just having a nap and for the first time ever she didn't hear the phone!' Tash said. 'Thank goodness, eh?'

Albie managed a smile. 'Yeah!'

'Come on, let's sort these out.' Tash started unwinding a pink ribbon from two sticks. 'Oh, and another thing! You know I've already got two tellies downstairs?'

'Yeah?' Albie had always wondered why she wanted to win another one.

'Well,' Tash said. 'I've got one in my bedroom, too!'

Albie looked her straight in the eye. Was she boasting now? Three televisions?

'The thing is . . .' Tash went on, 'I never wanted to win a telly. I was going to give you all my sticks to help *you* win.'

Albie sat up. 'What?' He grinned at her. 'I don't believe you.'

'No, really,' Tash said. 'They're all yours. Honest.'

'Why didn't you tell me before?' It didn't make sense. 'You feel sorry for me now, right?'

'No!' Tash shook her head. 'It was fun annoying you. I nearly told you a couple of times, then I thought, no, I'll wait to see how many you get. I wanted to see the look on your face. Sorry!'

'Huh,' Albie smiled. 'Well, I might forgive you one day!'

'Might? I've just counted my sticks,' Tash said. 'I've got over six hundred. There must be four hundred here we can rescue!'

Albie could have kissed her.

'Thanks,' was all he managed to say as she ran home to collect them.

* * *

They spent the rest of the evening rescuing lolly sticks. They straightened them, glued them, pulled off the transfers, unplaited pony manes from them and finally counted them out three times.

'One thousand exactly,' Tash said, tightening the top of the black bin bag. Albie taped the postcard with his name and address on the side and the next morning at nine o'clock sharp they handed it in at the entrance of Hill's Ice-cream unit on the Heveling Industrial Estate. The doorman seemed a bit surprised when he took it from them, but he didn't say anything.

* * *

It was two weeks later that Albie and Tash

understood the reason for the doorman's surprise. They were drinking lemonade in the kitchen when a Hill's Ice-cream lorry pulled up outside 23 Churchill Road. They both ran to the front door where a small man in a black suit stood smiling.

'I'm Mr Hill. Are you Albie Tilek?' he asked.

'That's me!' Albie opened the door wide. Mr Hill seemed shocked. He kept staring at Albie, as if it was impossible for him to have done it.

'You collected a thousand lolly sticks?'

'Yes,' Tash flicked her black, tangly hair behind her ears. 'He did and I helped. Go on. HAS HE WON A TELLY?'

'Actually, you did very well, lad,' Mr Hill hesitated for a moment. 'But we only had one entrant.'

'So,' Albie froze, 'I knew it. You cancelled the competition?'

'By law,' Mister Hill smiled, 'we must give you all four televisions, all four first prizes!' Tash caught Albie as he fell back and almost fainted clean away.

'Do you mind having your photograph taken?' Mr Hill asked.

* * *

Mum got the biggest shock when she came home.

'Where on earth did that come from?' She stood back, startled at the sight of the huge, wide-screen television taking up all the space on the kitchen table.

'I'll tell you in a minute,' Albie laughed. 'I've got a few things to show you first.' He led her by the hand into the living room, where another television exactly the same as the last one stood beside the gas fire.

'Blow me! What the . . .?'

'Don't say anything yet, Mum.' Albie led her up the stairs to her bedroom. 'Trust me!'

'Eeeek, eeek!' Tash followed them, giggling hard. There, on the chest of drawers, another wide-screen television.

'Now, Albie,' Mum started, 'what's going on?'

'Wait just a minute,' Albie grinned. 'There's only one more.'

'Only one more!' Mum gasped, staring at the last television taking up all the floor space in Albie's bedroom. Then he handed her the *Heveling Weekly News* and pointed to the competition details.

Mum read them quickly. 'The first four children to collect a thousand lolly sticks?'

'He was the only one who did it,' Tash said. 'They had to give him all four tellies. Can you believe it?'

'You collected over half for me!' Albie reminded her. 'And we didn't even know the prize tellies had surround sound, headphone sockets and super zoom.'

'Well, I never,' Mum collapsed on Waffle dog who was asleep on the bed. He let out one of his special Force Ten Waffle smells.

'Er . . . disgusting,' Tash fled the room holding her nose, followed by Albie, Mum, and Lucy shouting: 'Where's *my* telly? Ponies like watching telly!'

'You can share mine!' Albie picked her up and gave her a piggy-back down the stairs.

By August 16th, not only did Albie Tilek have four amazing televisions in his house, he was in the *Heveling Weekly News* twice: one page had a large photo of him playing the clarinet and looking like a pop star and another had a huge photo of him shaking hands with Mr Hill, accepting his four first prizes. He was the most famous kid in the whole of Heveling. Complete strangers came up to him and patted him on the back as if they were old friends.

The following week Big Malco ran up to him in the park, holding out a magazine. 'Hey, mate, have you seen this competition?'

'No.' Albie read the details to win a computer

games system. 'Wow, that sounds great!'

'I'm going to do it,' Big Malco smiled. 'I've entered four other competitions today. One's for a fantastic bike! And I've got to make up a poem to win a trip to Florida. Can you give me a hand, mate?'

'Yeah, okay!' Albie laughed.

'Oh, and sorry I nearly got you into trouble,' Big Malco said. 'We were only mucking about. We didn't steal anything from Casey's Computer Services. We just climbed over the wall to see if there were any spare games lying around. Then we got caught. I'm not doing that again. Scared the living daylights out of me.'

And then it happened. Albie walked up to Tash's house, lifted the brass door knocker to the highest limit and let it fall with a thud.

Tash opened the door and before Albie even said hello, it just came right out of his mouth: 'Will you be my girlfriend?'

'Eeek, eeeeeeeek,' Tash pushed him. 'It took you a long time to say that. 'Course I will, silly. Come in.'

'I can't move!' Albie said.

'Shocked I said yes?' Tash flashed her wriggling tadpole eyes.

'Er . . .' Albie grinned. 'You're standing on my foot!'

About the author

I always loved reading. Not just books: signposts, lolly sticks, tickets, everything! I kept it a big secret that I wanted to write a book until one day I had a story in my head that wouldn't go away – so I wrote it down. I was fourteen at the time and the story was about a girl who lived in a city and wanted to train a sheep dog.

I thought up *Lolly Woe* when I met a boy who desperately wanted to win a competition. He didn't think he had a chance but then a very extraordinary thing happened. Perhaps if you read this story you can guess what that was!